Volume 119 of the Yale Series of Younger Poets

Bees, and After

John Liles

Foreword by Rae Armantrout

Yale
UNIVERSITY PRESS
New Haven and London

PUBLISHED WITH ASSISTANCE FROM
A GRANT TO HONOR JAMES MERRILL.

Yale University Press books may be purchased in quantity for educational, business, or promotional use. For information, please e-mail sales.press@yale.edu (U.S. office) or sales@yaleup.co.uk (U.K. office).

Set in Yale type by Motto Publishing Services.
Printed in the United States of America.

ISBN 978-0-300-27941-2 (hardcover : alk. paper)
ISBN 978-0-300-27942-9 (paperback : alk. paper)
Library of Congress Control Number: 2024943404
A catalogue record for this book is available from the British Library.

This paper meets the requirements of ANSI/NISO Z39.48-1992 (Permanence of Paper).

10 9 8 7 6 5 4 3 2 1

Dedicated
to my grandmother and best friend
Cecelia Palmer

and
the Great Oxidation Event

Contents

Foreword

The poems in *Bees, and After* demonstrate a way of being in the world as one creature among equals. They sing this world in all its stinging power and scary vulnerability. Liles opens himself up to critics who might say he commits what used to be called the "pathetic fallacy," reading "human" feelings into the natural world. That kind of labeling is dated, I think, as recent studies have greatly enlarged the concept of sentience to include more and different creatures. (Fish, for instance, will count objects in experimental tasks and can be taught to discriminate between different types of music!) In this book feeling isn't confined to a single, privileged perspective.

Like an old-time naturalist, John Liles is in love with the organic (and inorganic) forms he finds in archives and in the field. I can't think of another poet writing today so dedicated to the close-up study of nature, though Forrest Gander and Arthur Sze come to mind as possible comparisons. One thing that makes Liles's work unique is that almost all of the poems in *Bees, and After* are intimate addresses to inhuman others. He is especially attuned to the small, the things we take for granted or don't notice at all: the woodlouse with "her flimsy mouth," the runt of the litter, and the lampshell brachiopod on its "struts and ribbons." The word choice here suggests not only small size, but fragility. If you were standing on a bridge supported by struts and *ribbons* you would, no doubt, be anxious to get off. The way Liles addresses and invokes these beings is tender, empathetic, and sonically gorgeous, but never sentimental. Because he views the world in close-up, not from a safe distance, he sees what we have in common with other creatures. After all, "we go / somewhere / animal / to die."

Bees, and After doesn't generally focus on the dangers confronting the biosphere—the toxicities and the climate crisis. However, the title points to these things, and there are other subtle references too. The poem "Without Which," which perhaps addresses a bee-keeper or perhaps even a bee hive, begins,

a planet to mend, you lend honey bees

:

kindred ignitions

into the blue
        unforgiving

I love the music of the vowels in these lines, especially the short i's, as well as the surprising power suggested by "kindred ignitions" as the swarm takes to the sky with its "unforgiving" atmosphere.

Although Liles writes most often in the second person, he does occasionally use other pronouns—even the first-person singular—but in these poems, identities and identifications morph unpredictably so that one entity collapses into another. The following passage from "Facula" begins with the speaker's very human perspective and from there slides obliquely into an identification with the moth he's describing:

I've been taught to love
and poke with a stick

dead reckoning : moths tend
headlong into the light

fanatic, to blossom fixation
(and who you thought was the moon)

. . . //

unable to reach you
I am unable to reach you

One can glimpse a possible narrative behind these lines. On seeing a moth that looks like it might be dead, a person pokes it to see if it moves. Perhaps that's what's happened, but it hardly matters. The juxtaposition of "love" and "poke with a stick" is so telling and jarring; it points beyond any plausible scenario to the human treatment of "nature" in general. Is poking with a stick a form of "dead" reckoning—using an instrument to gauge one's distance from some object? Such instrumental reason seems like the opposite of the moth's "fanatic" rush toward light, its "blossom fixation." But the next line is a kind of hinge: "(and who you thought was the moon)." Who is this "you"? Possibly the moth and yet, the use of "who" points in a new direction. It tips our reading toward something interpersonal, subtly setting up the later line "unable to reach you I . . ." The speaker identifies in himself a moth-like fixation, its fluttery desperation fully transferred to the one who began so coolly, poking with a stick. As the moth can't reach the moon, the speaker can't reach some thing, some *who,* that shines for him. It's not really possible to maintain a stick's distance from the world. "I" is (famously) "another."

While he often writes about creatures, Liles addresses the inorganic too. The first poem in the book, "Solar Photon," is, as the title suggests, about the force carrying particles of light which, here, demonstrates a dual nature. On the one hand, the "sunlight//enraptures sugar/simple starches/in a floral body." On the other, its "energetic collapse" will "break/the body to burn." Several of these poems are about—addressed to—minerals, some radioactive. Torbernite, which is a kind of copper, is taken home because it glows in the dark where it will "gunsling neutrinos//lung-cancerous radon particulates."(It's worth noting that not all the beings Liles invokes, from bees to minerals, to light itself are reliably helpful or kind. There is nothing Disneyesque in his idea of the natural world.)

John Liles doesn't have a "point" to make, at least not a simple one. He is a necessary poet now because he is in love with this world and he has taught himself to really see it. No one else would describe the crystals aligned within minerals as

> . . . delegates without
> exception
>
> at a perfect
>
> standstill
>
> matters
> of protocol

It's as if Liles is fondly teasing the crystals for their propriety, their well-behaved immobility. He talks to them, as to other beings, as one family member (or one lover) to another.

Bees, and After presents a participatory world in which we are not strangers. I'm grateful that he has given us what he calls, "my animism/this iffy rigorous hysteria." Such speculative precision is where science meets art.

These poems introduce a new kind of polyamorous lyric in which the idea of the "beloved" is expanded to include rock crystals and wood lice, a new form of elegy in which we praise and mourn the fragile world itself.

Rae Armantrout

Bees, and After

Solar photon

*

an elementary
massless force carrier
is intercepted
and at light speed

goes disposed
into a thimbleful
of body fluid

chloral pigment bundles of catalytic
quantum velocity brought
down

the planet's
fastest landing
in the small

of a fenestral open
within a cell's
organelle

*

the core-born god quantum
astral spillage let split

light-speed ungraspable nothings
and yet the leaflets

they strike—daughters
of daughter cells
pigment mitten

soft cushion
and flinch a
photon's gentle

velocity
straight to bed
to reiterate its

energetic collapse : break
the body to burn,

butcher, and backbone
an atmosphere's carbon
the sunlight

enrapturing sugar,
simple starches
in a floral body

Without which

a planet to mend, you lend honey bees
:
kindred ignitions

into the blue
unforgiving

to persist scintillas, to spark open wax
and induce
the workhorse's engines

hailing baby-faced and yellow-bellied bombardments
who masticate blossoms

gristle and grasp

and this is how we survive
this

oh unending animal,
you go where
the light goes

The steady state

this oh what a while
we've been given

to breathe the air
we breathe

that we form bonds
how we lend electrons,

something dearest
through the blue

to breathe the air
we breathe and in

the lungs
what bleeds

our honey alights
our hearts

and none of us
will endure this

Half-Life
(quartz)

and committed a
rock crystal
by shearing this historical
lithograph :

body parts paralleling
at sundown,
conifers
in rank and upright
against an agatized landscape

the daylight
rusted
down

ocular accidentalists
trying

not to slip

Quartz (SiO_2) is a hard, crystalline form of silica, with well-established crystals typically forming as a druse (a layer lining a void). Of all the common constituents of igneous rock, it is the most stable, the last to weather.

Half-life
(okenite)

void fillings
in loosely
oblate masses:

hand packed cotton
mouthed cavities

and delegates without
exception

at a perfect

standstill

matters
of protocol
gone

quieter

than ever
intended
after all
habitable
comforts

have been occupied

Okenite ($CaSi_2O_5 \cdot 2H_2O$) is a silicate, generally found as clusters of white, fibrous, radiating "cotton ball" crystals with basalt geodes.

Half-life
(opal)

*

in the body rotten mammalian
carcass night-whiled
of its molecules

you are honey soft,
hang dogged,
making embrace

*

what you undergo, crystalling :
lattice of laminates dizzy-getting
the bright sides into
a band gap, unpassable

go discoherence and backslide
with no discernable structure, you
nothing like other, hold
for a moment
one body of light

Opal (SiO_2+nH_2O) is a hydrated and amorphous form of silica, the spheres of which are so closely packed that no discernable crystal structures are found. The colorplay associated with opal occurs through the interference and diffraction of light as it passes through lattices of microstructured silica.

Half-life
(calcite)

*

the most stable chalk polymorph :

a poor amorphous precursor goes
down dry and loses

everything

as calcite reciprocates
this endpoint

*

stalagmitic brush hushed a sea sponge
cemented in a long while
dissolute cold co_2
touch

to shelters gradually removing
themselves from the situation

the occupied fossilizing
microstructures to bed
the dead present

Calcite ($CaCO_3$), a carbonate, is the most stable polymorph of the common calcium carbonate. It is often the primary constituent of exoskeletal structures in marine organisms, ranging from bivalves and echinoderms to sponges and red algae.

Salt sifting

exoskeletal hold-structure,
calcification of cuticle

the body is bundled under
tight junctions of radiating plaques
(polymer and protein) spatially
coordinated to points of contact,
coming to hinges with spent cuticle

shell growth necessitates an amassment
of calcium sourced first from sea-water,
but lacking proper salts the crab
calls to swoon his deader edges,
consumes the calcite slake

back inwards, opposite the heart
and stomach lumen, sponge
tissue through and re-attuned
sit gizzard stones—the bricks
a body makes its body its body wall

held spare in empty space,
gathered gastroliths are quick-dispersed,
chitin calcifying through
the void, and with plans
of sinking deeper,

Some decapods store calcium (for future shell repair and growth) in the form of small stones tucked between their heart and stomach walls.

the shell withstands unceasing
atmosphere, one full ocean
under a crab has kept
a promise—ionic flutters,
in every breath, free-floating
through a larger body

Abalone
(shell)

*

linchpin shell muscle
amending through pores
reamed in the outer edge
of the shell, highly fouled

her steady foot
withering as she,
harboring
an intestinal fluke
must turn
to her own
muscled body
to stave off
starvation,

self-atrophied and losing
hold

*

the iridescence of the nacre
is a result of light broken
at depths, diffracted and collected

the shell forms a blister
in response to a boring parasite,
worm or sponge, an overlapping

calcite cyst, a pearl sack,

trauma at the point of luster

Nimbus crush

*

fatigue toxins form
from the destruction of protoplasm
in a working muscle

body wastes want removed

cells tizzy,
rest

your worry is your work:
the moonturn

encradled
tidewhile
lowing

your mercy verbals
your mornform carbon

and how unendingly

abrasions

reach the bone

*

your body aches : nerve cells enduring
whiplash while you're lapsing
an ion or two :

glister,   whirligig-like-grapple,

you can't punish the dust

abouting you, wide-stance
hunched and one-twoing
and my
            oh-lucky-stars

I go outloud

just brought you home

and look at you   with those
flashbulbs

you really are brighter

I say

before realizing   it was your
skin

in the air

having ripped

its way

free

from your body

After-year

heliotrope bewildered : everywhere

the day
grows shorter
with some daphnes lacking darlings

you happenstance your animals—hereafter no humming bird,
beetle, or bombyx
            fluster
your
untouched
              calyx
            sugar-sore

with no one to gnaw on

your vital organs

you live your only summer

Dog spark

*

least gestated animal : littlest wisp of the
litter

a mother can only helpmate

so much

a son might give up

the muscle

and before his mother beg

analepsis

you are milk-hungry all your siblings bully

you are never in-latch

we all live a lifetime : you
survive yours entirely

but not everyone gets to eat

*

pup how you open your yellows

newborn, your nascent unknowing in

all your light
is starvation

a runt gets long-armed,

destitute in an only   yours   while all your
siblings

grow up to be dogs

foggy arcana of hunger : a riptide's distant fatigue

in a matter of somatics

and pup how could you know
any better
that this
is the only

going

we can dig a littlest
grave,

a palm-sized hollowing,

our hands in the dirt

when a little bright gives to dying :

when a dog

comes hungering

down

Emergency for

oh what the ask is

when I jab my little
brave at the body
ocean-shored

to anticipate the particulars
to see a bird so clear
in the light

sundress, sundress,
you are so far away

dismightying fright—life
light
blue molecular blue in a body,
body sized

what to trust under
an atmosphere

when animal, even you
don't know where to touch me

Amnesic shellfish poisoning

off-hand allelopathy of an algal
metabolite : diatomaceous

toxin slag that shellfish assemble
through filter feeding

when consumed, becomes
symptomatic in the mammal :

calcite excitations that burn
neurons into dementing

involuntary limbics, temporal blows,
motor degenerates and the memories

sequelae bloom

Produced by the diatom (Pseuo-nitzchia sp.), domoic acid is a biotoxin that can accumulate in filter feeders consuming this naturally occurring algae. Though it causes systemic poisoning in birds and mammals, the toxin seems to have no effect on mollusks.

Stone crinoid, sea lily

granular habitats stamped :

while awaiting
affectations of
pollen baskets,

hillsides of lilies held
a calyx gone cold

pistiless floral receptacles
who fell,
fossilized

seemingly patient
suspension feeders

might be starving
with nowhere else
to go

Within the class of Crinoidea, sea lilies are a sessile animal, consisting of a holdfast, a stem/stalk, and a crown of feathery arms. Amassments of ancient sea lilies are a common find in the fossil record, as the bone-like ossicles of the animal's stem readily endures the timeline to fossilization.

Cardiac knotting

the heart will have no interruption,
begins as a simple tube
(blood flow undivided)
at the middle of embryo
hurried—task of branching sufficient blood
levels into all upcoming situations

the heart, quick, outgrows its own
allotted cavity, and bends a branch righ
and back, pivots into
the cardiac loop, plotting
pistons, to hang self-knotting,
strung-up, the blood muscle must
raise divisions—the hollow heart

now split, turns intrinsic, walling out
a partition, a pocket, a sinus to house
the pulmonary hinges—a body's
bloodlines soon become confluent
to enter the heart

when later more transitional twisting
has caused a furrow, external,
the interfacing ventricle wall will
thicken—meshwork of muscular
fetters tuck together, reach out,
near-bridge for the atrial pacemaker

The heart is the first organ to form, beginning as a simple tube before following a distinct and self-driven blueprint to become the fully functioning four-chambered engine that we're all using to breathe.

an intra-arterial hollow so self-established
meanwhile, against the narrower walls
and paired opposite, loose masses
of migratory tissue driven—could linger on,
the non-particular life of a stem cell

nut here soft commotion reaching out,
endocardial cushions obstruct the blood
rush into opposite corners—predestined axes
of embryo, peristalsis in a pre-valved hollow,
the body's first organ to engine
an animal's ontogeny—the heart
as it begins to beat

With

all of us

surviving,

stay,

respirate,

everyone

must

breathe

together

everyone
must breathe

Half-life (forsterite)

*

marshal, magnesium
olivine end-member

domineering the mid matter,
local tectonics caught

lockjawing, historics of
an innate cosmic draw:

a new glow, gone long

with celestial bodies,
collaborative ballistics,

and falling into
newborn stars

first attuning
their atmosphere

or outloud and otherwise abundant,
two-thousand miles deep

Forsterite (Mg_2SiO_4) is the end-member (magnesium rich) of the olivine solid solution series. Below the crust, forsterite-rich olivine is the most abundant mineral in Earth's upper mantle.

Half-life
(animal)

*

a heart is entirely
something that stops,
a dog dies every day

the lithic forgiving
you back home

just come back
home

*

the dead lunge
of intonation, and
you get your
knuckles dusted

everyone gets nuzzled
down, dirt cozy,
disarticulations from your
once-living body

you're an animal,
you give your atoms back

Audible heart efforts

a sudden backflow
of blood rebounds, red
bounce about
both AV valves

each inlet articulate
when shut: sound off
of in-transit cells
sent adjacent and against
hesitant same-tissue

sound results out
from commotive closure:
pulmonary retrievals
and the valves that shut

systolic end-run response,
semi-lunars in embrace
catch colliding blood

red cells against
body-walls that settle
the excessive effort

of blood flow, breath
accidental, out loud

There are two normal heart sounds in a healthy human animal, caused by the turbulence created when the heart valves shut and the blood rebounds. The first is from the closing of the atrioventricular valves, and then the semilunar.

the removal
of an electron

from donor
to acceptor

respiration

is a process
of reduction

Restful amyg

I have it easy, leaving,
and I can't tell you this

but yours
is a lifetime

our fixations
unmatter

you'll forget
where you've

buried
these bones

*

ours is
a disaster
an animal I
flex into a dark so
easy and I'm
waiting for
this too

my nowhere while
you exhale
and
I exhale
atoms

and you breathe
and I breathe
but one of us
just wants the dirt
to die in

Astral bodies

movements

of salt
and salt bodies

into one wincing,

more

I dress for your comets : look to the dark

to hold close a body
on a way back home

and my knowing better

but I longpaw

your brightside

in the night

Among others

aperture, appetitive, my very stable
  nowhere

for a light to horizon

ecliptic   the moon

to mutualize
(a resonance)

I'm
nowhere
nearest

and then
  you

  look
right at me

Head lost illuminating

voltage-gated pathways are depolarized
and pore-forming membrane proteins
allow calcium influx from adjacent solutions

(cell insides become saturated)

excitation is mossy fiber running
southbound head-stems and paired shoots
through once-relaxed tissue

*

you've established rules,
preventative measures :

gut-principles and patterns
of self-reflection lost
in the feeling that

you are held to
head noise and further
itches. say it's all
removable

and lose it

*

head lost illuminating
small thoughts each concurrent
unoccurring moment hoped,

just wishing this warm attention

throw out
teeth for it

insist on restarting
the sore spots

*

involuntary and won't down-regulate,
particular defenses are stress-receptor
bound fidgets and the feeling follows

but the cortisol is excessive, hyperactive
little amygdala leaps and pounces
predispose biological tiffs
as tragic—you shout and scrape in
attendant panic

*

adrenal genesis of the headspace is sympathetic

the capacity to panic is self-contained

you receive stimuli and suffer
response :

emotional force across synapses
to a target cell, this end-point you
wallow to, feel
further but can't
reach

Facula

emotions are glowing dog carcasses
I've been taught to love
 and poke with a stick

dead reckoning : moths tend
headlong into the light

fanatic, to blossom fixation
(and who you thought was the moon)

the size of the world in the dark
uncertain and unable to speak and
unable to reach you
I am unable to reach you

honey and honeysuckle
(my heart in your lap)

Paired into our chance at this

so split, loose connective aggregates
of reticulate tissue and ground
providing (non-cellular) support,
mesenchymals will migrate

by signal sent, precursor cardiacs
extend their leading edge eager
and attaching to all felt surfaces

at cell-rear these adhesions
are uncoupled and stress-fiber
bundles tug the trailing edge
along in this collective direction

embryonic phenomenal: the heart
does stitch itself together
from its paired condition

opposite body walls and cavities
face-down, young embryo spilt
over the yolk surface

bud-structures beginning
destitute about the blastula,
our surviving animal must
embark as series of foldings

The heart is the only singular organ that forms from a paired condition, beginning split in two atop the surface of the yolk, before stitching itself together in the process of embryonic development.

the homebody hollows out
safe spaces and holds
to the heart, hung up
in the hot-start of all effort:

hopeless and without
the chance for new ambition

Paraphrasis

the less digestible
second-hand
            hand-sugar

and a host-bone's
syntaxis of dust

predatory complications arise
without a soft option

and every tiny dying

(just to make ends meet)

*

lasting
and ephemeral
physical contacts

manifesting specificity between

two charged forces :

to inhabit your nearnesses

(without doing harm)

Woodlouse

long-lived, slow growing
a woodlouse and her flimsy mouth

legging through loam and leaf litter
culling cellulose from the pulp

collecting in her hindgut;
consumption affords growth

soft-body pressure sheds her cuticle
fleshy back cracks through

but catching this, a louse turns
carnivorous coming after the sound

sequestering carbon from
the living cycle

Birds
(in their places)

Small bowls
worked into the rock face

ember and char littered,
stacked shells who've been newly
uncoupled from a home muscle

their calcite habits unheld
belly-up, a brickwork
of twinned crystal:

flat nacreous
death snaps of shine
and an underside
denying light

incidents of color shifts
censuring the honest
animal underbody

unfit for this situation,
the shell reflects
its seen perspective

humans who've arrived here
in awe corpses,
sunlight perverting

skeletons, and
the sight of those
who've spilled this

the white birds
turning each piece
over each bird stiff
legged, uneasy
near the heat

Contusionist

a moth takes
so many
short whiles
into the light

dazzling, dalliance, spore

divine :   "being"

in the world

(oh lucky stars)

spotlit
you
were
my
every
recovery

About a biome

*

synonymous and common studies
of muscle : bees in a hive

ten-thousand half-sisters blitzing
their luminescent embrace

militant touch-and-goers holding on
to all the lit in-betweens

golden ragdolls, daffodil-gasping
the pollen long armfuls and armfuls

this labor
of every small lifetime spent

*

the obligatory metabolic
demands of an animal, airborne

to run hemolymph through the heart
and water muscle

disa or daisy, forsake
these dainty arthropods

sashay your fractals anyhow,
phototroph : our atomic backbone

senescing,
some soon tomorrow

some fleshbright corollas
just go untouched

aspirated lastborn,
now

you can come back down
to the dirt

Longshot

scout :

one single bee to mesmer the iterative
soft-body waggle center-stage,
to step vector, shake,

and display her eights

one animal dancing exactness, and that
this can make our day :

directing the aperture of every likewise
animal

saying : half-sisters,
here is our next

abundance—milk vetch or tansy

today's daystart : save our maybes

(in this necessity for someone to speak up)

The waggle dance is used by honeybees to communicate the distance, direction, and abundance of flowers.

Next of kin

Pollinating insects resonate
professionally,

escorting their spark
into each floral avowal,

infallible units lasting
one half lunation in the daylight

work-bees who won't take blessing,
who'll have just one bee-size of honey

to masticate each next
deep lasting puncture

little sisters seed the gullet,
phenoms slur

into an ecotone

Just us

*

jinxing acetyl-choline
to gnaw on
my always coyote

unable to
my unable to

my animism,
this iffy rigorous hysteria
so yellow—disrepair   itive,
               phospho
lipids where
the heart goes
afferent, where
I am someone
to touch

*

un-down-regulated
acid mediative or
the preoccupant
intra-personal
escortments,

voltage unheld
dendritic cohabit,

synaptics to give,

we get, plummet

*

earnest the escape product
manic-ed my animal starved for
my animal

everywhere
mortal, or a ruthlessness
                                        delivered

melliferous scintilla eventide

            unlatch : each mortal
birth

this   biological   endgame

                         and here I go

            unholding

            every

            petal

Half-life
(torbernite)

by alliteration of pitchblende
and pretend we sent for the moon

less-planetesimal fluorescent
body in an apple-green patina

because the copper went phosphating
and the phosphate deluged

because you glow in the dark
and gunsling neutrinos

lung-cancerous radon particulates
and breathe easily out of the blue

but we bring you home, upright decay-chain
watch you half-life watch you daughter out

isotope of chernobyl respectralling mothlike
this touch-me-here while we keep you

away from our children

Torbernite $Cu[(UO_2)(PO_4)]_2(H_2O)_{12}$ is a relatively common radioactive hydrated green copper uranyl phosphate, found as a secondary mineral in the oxidation zones of uranium ore.

And goes the light

*

the obligatory metabolic demands of an animal
airborne

to run hemolymph through the heart and water
muscle

reciprocals an engine left open and the anti-freeze
lacking

nectar heartthrob until

you've booted all of it

*

bout : varroa downer

a quiver getting
the oh-little-anymores

spring meantime bleeding,
this hard ash and gawk

(to survive what gets said in the dark)

*

heart-felt and latticed
hopelike ignitions

landed

local florets boomed

bees come home
holding all they can

*

we are tiny mothers

without
any

oxygen

to spare

Lampshells
(brachiopods)

A step through shallow water
and huddled in the dark small
shells sheltering their decisive systems

*

a thin fold of the body extends to enclose
a cavity, a canal : Inarticulate, or not connected

by tooth-and-socket structures – a mouth
supported by skeletal struts and ribbons

inward from a narrow lip tucked
into the feeding column confluent

with the wet catches of breath and errant
bantams, biomasses

babies born as such small drifters,
long-term crawlers coalescing

with passing phototrophs sinking
to the sea floor when shells grow heavy

Brachiopods, occupying a phylum distinct from mollusks, fall into two categories: articulate, and inarticulate. Rare and non-metamorphic, the larvae of the inarticulate form as functioning, miniature adults. These larvae then swim through the water for many months, feeding, until the moment their shell becomes heavy enough to sink to the bottom, to live the rest of their lives as sessile adults.

My knowing better

pre-satellitic the moon was
just material, sub terrain

and iron we untouched until
found aerolites landed

when the heart meets her
myocytes, she's electric

comets come out of the dark
back home

every so often in the night
I look up

and hold out

to be a behavior of atoms

(or their underpinnings)

“but most hopes are private and flicker”

How to ask anyone near

*

nearness brings us not to
measure our handfuls

when you've been hungry
for long enough

there is no summation
able

to keep your body

away

from the body

it eats

*

enthusiasm can incapacitate
in the companion animal

what could make bearable
all that we must

sugar incantations,
snuggest lifemates,

arteries

are endless

until they aren’t

*

and when the dark goes down

and you are photon-lonely

there is no way
to approximate

that touch

Parastasis

*

acoustic
communication

within a species

(song)

*

solving
a single bee's

statement

into the sunlight

and to arrive
at flowers

*

hungry
and utterly

light
dependent

we stay

as long
as we can

*

words but
the distance
situates
          -isms

the approachable body
I just want
          to let

you in

before
we go
somewhere
animal

to die

*

sweet
unendurable
massacre

the earth
rotates

and without
your roar

we are
not well
equipped

to handle
any of this

My hound

*

unamenable :

the living feverfew
earth-captive animals,
their every innateness
displaced until
ending and into

disaster : to wake up

so clearly this
sister species
othered and
articulating
just one molecular
collection

(mine)

*

to hear a bird so clear in the distance
to awake and find egg-whites

my hidden girlish riblet glowing just one-half lunation
my moment of hope

but the ambit glances :

some shore birds might never
find the ocean

*

microsocial empathy contagions
of affective resonance

in a still becoming true
sentence

tinderbox, two flinches
from the sky, I try

to stay near

i want to ask for too much

a bird for your birdhouse

call me in
from the rough

*

half-buried dog-unwalked
animals in an unlit
immenseness

and I'm asking
my other
to stay near

as sometimes a light
goes down
into nothing,

and next to you
is every place
that I am

*

we are each of us glowing

open-hearted

far-away animals

rare

as a lifetime

bees

you could wish into the world

and over every living mousetrap

I am always

coming back home

to you

Acknowledgments

An expression of appreciation is owed to the editors of the following journals and magazines where the respective poems first appeared: Parataxis (The Journal); Solar photon and Half-life (animal) (filling station); Facula (Rust+Moth); Okenite, Cinnabar, Forsterite and other minerals (inter/rupture); The steady state and How to ask anyone near (ctrl + v); Emergency for (Juked), Myogenesis and the rest unsettled (decomP); Birds in their places (Gulf Stream Review); Abalone (Arcadia), and Contusionist, Quartz, Asterodea, and Opal (Clip).

For the material support, the time and space to write, and the absolute human kindness, thank you to all those involved with the Oak Spring Garden, and with the James Merrill House, at a time when I so desperately needed the feeling of home. As well, this book would not have happened without my time in the NYU MFA program, and the support and patience of all those involved.

The quote "but most hopes are private and flicker" is from Joanna Klink, "Excerpts from a Secret Prophecy," *New England Review* 35: 4 (2015): 199–203.

Gratitudes

Immense and endless gratitudes to the humans and animals that facilitated the arrival of this book, both in choosing the words, and surviving this world, hard as it has been.

Ben Stillerman, Yanitsa Toneva, my parents Lisa and Jason, Kayla Lamb, Uncle Jimmy, Aunts Jimelle and Marsha, Adina, Grandma, Grandpa, and the whole Reavis family, my deepest love and gratitude for everything you have done for me in my life, innumerable and beyond name.

For my faculty/educators, Matt Rohrer, John Granger, Eliot Wirshbo, Catherine Barnett, Melvin Freilicher, Deborah Landau, Ivan Evans, Cole Swensen, Yusef Komunyaaka, Ben Doller, Anne Carson, Ms.Haydon, Ms. Bennett, Ms. Dolkas, thank you for your patience, your investment, and your continued contributions to your students.

My PEEC family and naturalist co-staff, Brook, Cypress, Oak Bark, Koala, Firefly, Cypress, Esme, Chris Williams, Lorrie Lagasse, and more, I hold you close in the present day, and my life is ever brighter for our time together.

Thank you to those who knew me young—to Daryl Henry, Teri Havener, the Golds, the Lazars, the Tidd family, Alton Caesar, Coach Mark, Eddie Vanderdoes, Coach Pruit—for the many times you kept me under a wing, took the time to help me along with my ambitions, and let me be a kid, safe.

Steph, Wanda, Billie, Ed, Hailey, David, Lisa, Nick—my dear neighbors, and those who loved my grandma so fiercely along the way—we never would have made it without you. And for my growing years and present head, thank you Felicia Gold, Tim Schools, Lizzie Holt, and Louis Lazar.

Know that I hold you dearly in my heart, appreciate you, and think of you often: Elizabeth Estella, Wally Ludel, Aria Aber, India Gonzalez, Charisma Price, Jao Young Lee, Natasha Rao, Leigh Sugar, Elissa Levy, Autumn Von Plinsky, Sam Smith, Claire Martin, Devereux Fortuna, Ben Blumstein, Marney Rathbun, TJ. Smith, Madeline Mori, Rachel Mannheimer, JJ Starr, Colin Dekeersgieter, Beata Kasiarz, EM Means, Ben Luton, Peter Geibel, Kit Schluter, Desiree Bailey, Lee Jasperse, Damaris Han, Noah Griefer, Dilprit Singh, Evan Dolly, Alaina Lamb, and my many supportive peers at UCSD. And my pups, Punkadelly, Blaze, and Jackson.

All of my students, with whom the days go by so brief, and feel so worthwhile.

And all the dogs I have ever known.